This book
belongs to

For Molly and Thomas

PENGUIN BOOKS

UK | USA | Canada | Ireland | Australia
India | New Zealand | South Africa | China

Penguin Random House Australia

Penguin Random House Australia is part of the Penguin Random House group of companies whose addresses can be found at global.penguinrandomhouse.com.

First published by Penguin, an imprint of Penguin Random House Australia Pty Ltd, in 2025

Printed and bound in Australia by Griffin Press, an accredited
ISO AS/NZS 14001 Environmental Management Systems printer

NATIONAL LIBRARY OF AUSTRALIA

A catalogue record for this book is available from the National Library of Australia

MIX
Paper | Supporting responsible forestry
FSC® C018684
FSC www.fsc.org

ISBN 978 1 76135 908 8 (Paperback)

penguin.com.au

We at Penguin Random House Australia acknowledge that Aboriginal and Torres Strait Islander peoples are the Traditional Custodians and the first storytellers of the lands on which we live and work. We honour Aboriginal and Torres Strait Islander peoples' continuous connection to Country, waters, skies and communities. We celebrate Aboriginal and Torres Strait Islander stories, traditions and living cultures; and we pay our respects to Elders past and present.

Cosy Fantasy

A COLOURING ESCAPE

Stephanie Whorlow

Sometimes we need a little
fantasy to escape reality.
So sit back, relax and let
your creativity fly . . .

COOK
Eyes
Bones
POTIONS
SPELLS
WITCHES
POISON
LOVE

Books

WINGS CAFE
Z Z Z Z
Cooking
OPEN

zzz

Books to go
ORDER HERE
Fantasy Bookstore

Magic